ABOUT THIS NO NONSENSE

SUCCESS GUIDE

This No Nonsense Success Guide, like each Success Guide, has been designed to live up to *both* parts of its name . . . to provide you with useful No Nonsense information *and* to increase your personal chances for Success!

Owning and operating a home-based business can be the best of *both* possible worlds: Taking control of your personal *and* professional life under the same roof!

Owning and operating a business from home requires imagination, dedication and organization.

HOW TO RUN A BUSINESS OUT OF YOUR HOME provides the basic information you need to succeed in pursuit of one of today's most exciting — and rewarding — self-employment opportunities!

THE NO NONSENSE LIBRARY

NO NONSENSE SUCCESS GUIDES

Getting Into the Consulting Business
Getting Into the Mail Order Business
How to Own and Operate a Franchise
How to Run a Business Out of Your Home
How (and Where) to Get the Money to Get Started
The Self-Employment Test

OTHER NO NONSENSE GUIDES

CAR GUIDES

CAREER GUIDES

COOKING GUIDES

FINANCIAL GUIDES

HEALTH GUIDES

LEGAL GUIDES

PARENTING GUIDES

PHOTOGRAPHY GUIDES

REAL ESTATE GUIDES

STUDY GUIDES

WINE GUIDES

NO NONSENSE

SUCCESS GUIDE

HOW TO RUN A BUSINESS OUT OF YOUR HOME

STEVE KAHN

LONGMEADOW PRESS

How To Run A Business Out Of Your Home

Cover design by Tom Fowler, Inc.

Composition by Tod Clonan Associates, Inc.

Published by Longmeadow Press, 201 High Ridge Road, Stamford. Connecticut 06904. No part of this book may be reproduced or used in any form or by any means, electronic or mechanical, including photocopying, recording, or by an information storage and retrieval system, without permission in writing from the publisher.

ISBN: 0-681-40125-7

Printed in the United States of America

0 9 8 7 6

TABLE OF CONTENTS

1

HOW TO MAKE THE DECISION TO START A BUSINESS AT HOME

The decision to start a home-based business — to begin a new business within walking distance of your kitchen! — will be your *second* decision as a new entrepreneur.

Your *first* decision will already have been made: The decision to become an entrepreneur and enter the fast-growing world of the self-employed. It is a decision which thousands of ambitious, confident people make each working day.

In fact, statistics project that between five and ten million Americans will own and operate home-based businesses by 1990!

As a home-based entrepreneur, you will be setting out on a journey designed to improve the overall quality of your life by taking control of your working life. It will be a journey filled with enormous challenges, unexpected obstacles . . . and the possibility of significant financial and emotional rewards!

You will have to make certain that you are endowed with confidence and with patience; that you are prepared to cope with the inevitable ups-and-downs which will occur as you build your home-based business, and that you have the support of all the people in your life who matter to you.

Every new business entails considerable risk, but you have already skewed the odds in your favor: *By electing to start your own new business at home, you will be beginning your self-employment career with the right attitude.*

Home-Based Benefit No 1:
Low Overhead

Accountants designate them as "fixed expenses." Experienced entrepreneurs have a less elegant description; they refer to it as "the nut." You and I would most likely refer to it as "overhead."

Whatever you call it, "it" is the sum of all those expenses which you have to pay each month *before* you produce a dollar's worth of revenues.

Such consistent items as heat, rent, telephone, office equipment maintenance, insurance premiums and license fees comprise this recurring category of business expense.

By starting your new business at home (where, presumably, the rent or the mortgage payment were already being paid long before you decided to go into business for yourself), you have succeeded in eliminating one of a business' most onerous "fixed expenses:" *The rent.*

Thus, you are starting out with an enormous financial (and even emotional) advantage. "Meeting the rent" is an awesome obligation for any business, particularly a new one. Landlords don't care about the fragile state of your business; their business is collecting rent, and they intend to collect yours every 30 days — whether or not you've made a single sale during the month.

Maintaining a low, efficient overhead is a sound, conservative business practice. Rent is frequently the largest single "fixed expense." By eliminating it, you have given your new business a significant advantage.

Home-Based Benefit No. 2:
Your Ego's In The Right Place

If you were to ask a venture capitalist (someone who funds new start-up enterprises) what single element causes him to back away from a prospective deal, he would probably tell you that it was an entrepreneur who ushers him into a large, flashy office — from which he then proceeds to attempt to convince the venture capitalist that he will prudently manage the money which he is seeking to raise!

The point is obvious: The intelligent entrepreneur has a strong sense of priorities. He knows that his limited funds have to be spent as carefully and productively as possible. His sense of personal satisfaction will come from the success of the business, not from the elegance of his high-rent (non-revenue-producing) corner office.

Perhaps one day, when the business is well established, he will provide himself with such a dividend. In the meantime, the smart entrepreneur is familiar with the classic story of Steve Jobs, who started a computer business in his garage. You may not be familiar with his name, but you most certainly know the name of the business which began in such modest surroundings: *Apple Computer!*

Home-Based Benefit No. 3:
Efficiency

If you live an hour from where you work, you spend two hours a day commuting. That's ten hours a week, 500 hours a year!

To the new entrepreneur, even more than most people, time *is* money. By working at home, you will be saving time *and* money. It is an irresistible combination.

All of your working hours will be productive ones, and your sense of purpose will be heightened. There is no more satisfying "bottom line," and working at home will provide you with that priceless sense of satisfaction every working day.

Home-Based Benefit No. 4:
Your Self-Discipline

One of the most critical characteristics of the entrepreneur is self-discipline. He has to be able to motivate himself, to provide his own sense of direction and determination. There is no "boss" or time clock to keep him in line.

Working at home demands enormous self-discipline because of the endless potential distractions. When you're working at home, you have to be able to resist the refrigerator, the television and even the easy chair in which you read the evening paper and watch *The Bill Cosby Show.* You have to walk past them all — *and get to work!*

You already have a healthy dose of self-discipline or else you wouldn't have decided to go into business for yourself. By working at home, you're putting that self-discipline to the test every working hour of every working day. It is a test which you cannot permit yourself to fail — and, therefore, it becomes another of the many subtle benefits of starting a home-based business.

Home-Based Benefit No. 5:
"Quality Time"

Sitting in front of a television set watching Vanna White move letters may be relaxing — but not even the biggest "Wheel of Fortune" fan would characterize it as "quality" time.

Sharing the day's events with your spouse, reading your child a storybook or preparing a business plan for a meeting tomorrow are more reasonable definitions of "quality" time.

The home-based entrepreneur quickly develops a useful sense of "quality" time — because he has to make time-based judgments all day long in the same environment where he works *and* lives.

"Quality" time is admittedly difficult to quantify but, like many positive events, most of us recognize it when it occurs. It is a dimension which can improve the quality of our lives — and the home-based entrepreneur often develops the ability to create it because he *has* to.

There are many reasons why the new entrepreneur decides to start his business at home. Sometimes, the reason is as simple and direct as the money. If he had to rent space, he couldn't afford to go into business in the first place.

Usually, however, the significant rent savings is only one of a number of reasons for making the decision to work at home. Typically, the home-based entrepreneur feels confident and comfortable in familiar surroundings and regards himself as sufficiently self-disciplined to be productive and creative despite the tempting distractions.

We have touched upon some of the benefits of establishing a business at home. Some are financial; some are emotional; all of them are real.

If they make sense to you, and if your home can handle the physical requirements of your particular business, then you are an ideal candidate for owning and operating a business at home.

2

HOW TO DEVELOP THE BUSINESS PLAN FOR YOUR HOME-BASED BUSINESS

The traditional business plan consists of four primary parts: (1) A careful definition of your business. (2) A marketing plan. (3) A production plan. (4) A financial plan. Together, they will serve as the blueprint for the growth and development of your home-based business.

Perhaps the most useful aspect of writing a business plan is that it is an exercise which makes you ask yourself all of the hard questions which an entrepreneur-to-be must consider *in advance* of going into business.

We will get into the specifics of each of these four basic areas, but first we are going to share two sets of questions with you. Each set has been developed by the U.S. Small Business Administration, commonly referred to as the SBA. (There is a complete list of SBA offices beginning on page 82, and you will be introduced to the SBA in detail in chapter 15.)

Requirements For Success

The SBA developed these three questions "to determine whether your idea meets the basic requirements for a successful new project." The SBA has grouped them together as "requirements for success" and says: "You must be able to answer *at least one* of the following questions with a 'yes.' "

(1) Does the product/service/business serve a presently unserved need?

(2) Does the product/service/business serve an existing market in which demand exceeds supply?

(3) Can the product/service/business successfully compete with existing competition because of an "advantageous situation," such as better price, location, etc.?

Major Flaws

Conversely, the SBA has developed these five questions to provide you with "an early warning system" of any "major flaws" in your proposed product/service/business. According to the SBA: "A 'yes' response to questions such as the following would indicate that the idea *has little chance for success.*"

(1) Are there any causes (i.e., restrictions, monopolies, shortages) that make any of the required factors of production unavailable (i.e., unreasonable cost, scarce skills, energy, material, equipment, processes, technology, or personnel)?

(2) Are capital requirements for entry or continuing operations excessive?

(3) Is adequate financing hard to obtain?

(4) Are there potential detrimental environmental effects?

(5) Are there factors that prevent effective marketing?

The SBA developed these general questions to "help you screen out ideas that are likely to fail *before* you invest extensive time, money and effort in them."

A "wrong" answer to a question in either set will not necessarily doom your business before it is born. However, at the very least, a "wrong" answer should encourage you to take another look at your prospective product/service/business.

Your Business Plan

The key word is *your.* You are writing about *your* prospective business, one which will shape *your* life, *your* future. Thus, your business plan is among the most important projects which you will ever undertake.

(1) Describe Your Business
It's difficult to imagine, but many would-be entrepreneurs don't really know what business they're going into. They *think* they know what the nature of their business is — *"advertising," "mail order," "computers," "catering," "pet products"* — but they don't have a specific, action-oriented definition of their prospective enterprise.

You cannot begin a new business unless you know exactly what business you will be in!

Thus, the key to the first section of your business plan is to develop a working description of your business. To establish the definition of your business, you should ask yourself specific items and questions such as these:

(a) Briefly describe the business you want to enter.

(b) List the products and/or services you want to sell.

(c) Describe who will use your products and/or services.

(d) Why would someone buy your products and/or services?

(e) List your major competitors — those who sell or provide similar products and/or services.

You must have a clear, focused vision of your new business. That vision begins with an unblurred ability to define and describe it without uncertainty or hesitation.

(2) The Marketing Plan

In the first instance, you have to analyze the market for your business in order to be able to make a realistic projection of sales. Then you will have to determine whether the market for your business is sufficient to sustain a profitable business. Again, the most useful technique is to ask yourself some very direct and unambiguous questions:

(a) What are consumers' attitudes towards businesses like yours?

(b) What do you know about consumer shopping and spending patterns relative to your type of business?

(c) Is the price of your product or service especially important to your target market?

(d) Can you appeal to the entire market?

(e) If you appeal to only a market segment, is it large enough to be profitable?

(f) Who are your major competitors?

(g) What are the major strengths of each?

(h) What are the major weaknesses of each?

(i) Have any firms of your type gone out of business lately?

(j) If so, why?

(k) Are your competitors' profits increasing, decreasing or stable?

(l) Can you compete with your competition?

You will need all this information in order to make some intelligent — and honest! — sales projections. You should prepare these projections on a month-by-month basis, matching up projected income with projected expenses. *Don't over-estimate your projected income or under-estimate your projected expenses!*

(3) The Production Plan

As we noted in the opening paragraph of this chapter, no section of your business plan will stand alone; a business plan is truly the sum — and substance — of its parts.

Once you have determined the size and shape of your market, you have to deal with the production of your product or service. Every product or service has specific needs which cannot be addressed in a general book; but, again, there are fundamental questions which virtually every prospective business needs answered:

(a) Can you make a list of every item of inventory and operating supplies needed?

(b) Do you know the quantity, quality, technical specifications, and price ranges desired?

(c) Do you know the name and location of each potential source of supply?

(d) Do you know the price ranges available for each product from each supplier?

(e) Do you know the sales and credit terms of each supplier?

(f) Will the price available allow you to achieve an adequate mark-up?

(4) The Financial Plan

Now that you know exactly what business you will be in, what your market is and what it will cost you to produce your product or service, you are in a position to make some realistic projections. The resulting numbers will become the basis of the financial section of your business plan.

Once you have determined prices for your products or services and the size of your market, you can estimate your monthly income. Be sure to make your projection as conservative as possible.

That monthly income — which, presumably, will grow on a healthy upwards curve as your business becomes established — will be offset by your operating expenses, which include everything you need to conduct your business. Your accountant can help you to make certain that you have not overlooked any "hidden" items.

This income vs. expense projection will provide you with the basic anticipated financial condition of your business.

It will give you an indication of when you can reasonably expect your business to become profitable.

If you anticipate making a profit in six months, be certain to have at least enough working capital on hand for a year!

Also be certain to compute your start-up expenses. These are one-time non-recurring expenses which you will incur as you begin your business — and will include everything from a telephone deposit to decorating expenses to the cost of printing announcements introducing your business to the world. Many new business owners overlook start-up expenses; remind yourself not to become one of them.

The primary purpose of the financial plan is to determine how much money you will need to begin and to sustain your new business.

You will, of course, also have to sustain yourself and your family during these early, cash-poor months.

Therefore, together with your business financial plan, you will have to plan for your personal expenses. This estimate should include all of your normal living expenses. *Obviously, you must plan for sufficient reserve capital to cover these expenses in addition to your business expenses.*

The Bottom Line

Hopefully, your business plan will confirm your expectations and enable you to proceed on schedule.

Occasionally, of course, a business plan — once fully prepared — brings some unexpected and unpleasant surprises.

If that should occur, you can take comfort in the knowledge that the business plan served one of its key purposes — alerting you to problems before they could really hurt you!

In both instances, the business plan will serve as the blueprint for your new home-based business and help you to make certain that the foundation for your business is as sound and as solid as it can be.

There are, of course, no guarantees for success even with the best of plans. Historically, however, successful entrepreneurs know that structures built on strong foundations have the best chances of surviving.

3

THE ADVANTAGES OF WORKING AT HOME

We touched upon some of the advantages of working at home in the first chapter. They included eliminating additional rent as an on-going burden and obligation for a new business; eliminating the time it formerly took to commute to an away-from-home office; challenging one's sense of self-discipline, which is a key to every entrepreneur's success; and creating "quality time" for the entrepreneur and his family.

Any one of these advantages alone could be compelling catalysts for making the decision to begin a new business at home; the purpose of this chapter is to suggest that it gets even better for the home-based entrepreneur!

Starting A Part-Time Business At Home

Starting any new business is a risk and an adventure into the unknown. Not until the new business owner is in business for himself will he really know what it feels like to be self-employed, to be his own boss.

Beginning a business at home enables the new entrepreneur to make that determination without risking everything: Many home-based businesses are started as part-time or "moonlighting" enterprises.

If the part-time, home-based business is successful, it can easily be converted into a full-time, home-based business.

If the part-time, home-based business does not meet expectations, it can be ended without causing the new entrepreneur any embarrassment.

He will not have to put a "For Rent" sign on his abandoned store or seek a sub-lease tenant for his vacant office space.

To all of us, home is where the heart is. To the cautious new entrepreneur, home is where the *start* is!

Exchanging Blue Suits For Blue Jeans

The home-based business has no dress code. The home-based entrepreneur can wear whatever he wants to.

This may seem like a minor advantage — and it probably is — but studies have shown that "dress for success" stress can be a real problem for some people. Working at home eliminates the problem — and can save a lot of wardrobe expense, as well.

Plus, many home-based entrepreneurs admit, they love the thought of working in blue jeans and loafers while their former colleagues are working in more traditional clothes.

Tax Advantages

We will devote an entire chapter to the tax aspects of the home-based business, so we will reserve the details on this significant advantage for that section of the book.

The tax benefits for all entrepreneurs are considerable; the tax benefits for home-based entrepreneurs are even more considerable.

Flexible Lifestyle

This is perhaps the ultimate advantage of working at home.

The home-based entrepreneur is not locked into a schedule established by arbitrary factors.

If he's an early bird, he can begin working before dawn.

If she's a night owl, she can work past midnight.

If he's a parent, he can call 3 o'clock "lunch" and have a snack with the kids when they get home from school.

You get the idea — and most home-based entrepreneurs love the idea!

Saving tax dollars is a quantifiable benefit.

Saving commuting time is a quantifiable benefit.

Living a flexible, self-determined, home-based lifestyle cannot be so conventionally quantified — because most entrepreneurs who work at home will tell you that this is the most priceless benefit of all.

However, nothing is perfect — not even working at home. The next chapter will give equal time to the *disadvantages* of owning and operating a business at home.

4

THE DISADVANTAGES OF WORKING AT HOME

There can be some disadvantages to working at home. However, virtually all of the problems which a home-based business can produce have solutions.

Distractions: From Diapers to Doorbells

The home-based entrepreneur is vulnerable to infinite distractions. Some are internal — like snack-filled refrigerators, wandering children and plump living room sofas asking to be sat in. Others are external — like personal phone calls, door-to-door salesmen and friendly neighbors who consider your car in the driveway as a signal that you're home *(not that you're home working)* and therefore fair game for a mid-day chat.

Some home-based entrepreneurs don't mind a few unexpected disruptions during the day. Most, however, make it a point to avoid counter-productive distractions: Children are given firm ground rules; refrigerators are ignored; personal phone calls are not accepted, and friendly neighbors are given a quick but polite lesson about "business hours."

The distractions will never be completely eliminated, but they can be successfully controlled.

Creating A Professional Image

Some new entrepreneurs worry about being able to create a credible professional image from within their home-based headquarters.

It is an understandable concern but one which can be overcome with a creative dose of imagination.

An organization's image typically comes from its products or services and its promotional materials.

The home-based business can establish a strong professional image with attractive letterheads, a strong graphic identity — and a product or service so good that buyers wouldn't even think about being concerned about the location of a business able to produce such high-quality work!

Additionally, the home-based entrepreneur should make it a point to keep his office and reception area (if he has one) as separate as possible from his living space. That separation, together with a business-like decor, will help to establish and maintain a positive professional image.

Isolation

This can be a serious problem. Working alone can be a stressful experience, especially for someone used to working in a busy, heavily-populated environment.

If isolation becomes a problem, the home-based entrepreneur has to schedule regular out-of-home breaks. It may simply mean going to the post office or meeting a client for lunch at a downtown restaurant. It may also mean that a home-based entrepreneur suffering from isolation has to establish a regular series of outside appointments — which will provide him with the anticipation and comfort he needs whenever being inside (alone) becomes unbearable.

An ideal solution — which solves the problem of isolation as well as the problem of staying fit while working at home — might be to join a health club and schedule a daily break there so that no working day will be without an out-of-house appointment.

Getting Motivated

It's hard enough (for many of us) to get up in the morning even knowing that an entire office, plant or store is expecting us.

It's that much harder when the journey between the bedroom and the workplace is *this close* — and the only one expecting you is you!

This problem is not the only potential problem caused by the proximity of your living space and your workplace. The whole idea of motivating yourself — without supervisors, co-workers and company-generated reminders to stimulate you — can be difficult to cope with.

You really have no options here: *You have to get up. You have to get down to work. You have to keep on working even without outside factors to spur you.*

All entrepreneurs need to have a strong sense of self-discipline. Home-based entrepreneurs (at least in the beginning) need a *super-sense* of self-discipline in order to succeed.

From Laws You Didn't Know Existed —
To Neighbors Who Didn't Know You Existed!

Most of the potential problems in this catch-all category are covered in later chapters. The home-based entrepreneur will soon realize that problems will come from areas which he didn't have to think about when his house was simply a home, not a home and office.

He didn't have to think about zoning laws; now he will have to not only think about them but meet their commercial requirements.

He didn't think about cranky neighbors; now he will have to deal with them when they keep calling the police because his customers' cars are spilling out of his driveway into the street.

The list is endless — and should be considered one of the start-up burdens of a new home-based business. The problems seem overwhelming at first but can usually be resolved by a show of good faith on all sides. There is no question, however, that successfully resolving them will require time, energy, diplomacy and patience on the part of the new home-based business owner.

If such problems should arise in your location, this thought will comfort you: *Your competitors may not be suffering from similar problems but they're paying rent and you're not!*

5

THE TYPES OF BUSINESS MOST SUITABLE TO A HOME-BASED ENTERPRISE

If, for example, your business deals with, art, antiques or animals, working at home will probably work out for you. If, however, you are thinking of a business which requires heavy equipment, heavy traffic or unconventional business hours, working at home — in a residential neighborhood — will probably not work for you.

Obviously, not every business lends itself to a home-based environment.

The good news for the prospective home-based entrepreneur is that the service industry is the fastest-growing segment of the economy, and most service businesses will probably thrive in a home-based environment.

You Don't Have To Become Self-Employed To Work At Home

This book is essentially directed to prospective entrepreneurs thinking of starting a business at home, either on a part-time or a full-time basis.

However, technological advances and more liberal employer attitudes are also making it possible for certain categories of workers to remain salaried employees while working at home.

It is almost "old news" that employees who have a computer-based position can work at home, at least several days each week. All they need is a home computer which is compatible with and linked to their employer's primary computers back at the office.

The good "new news" is that, as companies begin to understand that productivity is often higher from home-based employees, more and more of them are offering at-home opportunities for full-time salaried employees. Among the more common categories being afforded this option are analysts (financial, marketing, etc.), market researchers, editors, customer service representatives and even secretarial service providers.

Tax and other consequences are more complicated, and different from, the benefits available to self-employed entrepreneurs; so if you are contemplating this option, you will have to be briefed on the currently applicable rulings by your employer, your lawyer and your accountant.

How To Maintain A Home-Based Business Even When Part of Your Business Might Conflict With Neighborhood Standards

If, for instance, you are a sales representative who has to conduct a "major showing" annually, you need not be precluded from operating your business from home. You simply have to hold your annual display away from home, in a local hotel or in someone's office or (non-conflicting) showroom.

Even if you are going to be manufacturing a product, you can work out a situation whereby your home is "headquarters" — for billing, marketing, etc. — while the factory produces your merchandise.

Similarly, if your business requires the storage of materials or a large inventory of product, you can simply arrange for a warehouse or showroom elsewhere. This will, of course, add some measure of rent to your operating expenses — but warehouse and storage space is significantly less expensive than prime office space, so you will still realize considerable savings by conducting your business at home.

Two growing trends are working in favor of the home based businessperson.

(1) Most new businesses are service businesses, and most service businesses are suitable for home-based operations.

(2) As more and more at-home businesses are established — and neighbors who once might have objected to your home business are thinking about starting their own! — the occasional bias which currently arises in some situations will virtually dissolve as a threat to the establishment of such businesses.

In other words, if you are thinking about starting a home-based business, you are in the right place at the right time!

6

MAKING IT LEGAL: MEETING ALL THE REGULATIONS

The home-based entrepreneur will have to deal with all of the legal details which are required in any new business — plus certain specific requirements which are unique to a business operated from home.

Zoning:
Your House May Be A Home
But Is It A (Legal) Office?

Working in your house is a very different matter from just living in it. When you're simply living at home, there are no laws setting standards for what you should have for dinner or what you can watch on television. When you're working at home, the same authorities who don't care what you had for dinner or whether you watched "60 Minutes" or "The Sunday Night Movie" suddenly begin to take a great interest in your business.

In fact, there is a possibility that your business may not even be legally conducted from your home!

Fortunately, the SBA reports that "cultural and national trends point in the direction of zoning regulations that allow quiet, non-polluting, low-traffic kinds of home businesses."

Nevertheless, your first order of business *before* you begin your home-based business is to thoroughly investigate the zoning laws in your community. Zoning laws are those regulations which spell out activities permitted and prohibited in specific portions (zones) of a city or county.

Most areas of the country have Planning, Zoning and Appeals Boards. Go to your town hall, zoning office or local library to get a copy of the most updated zoning laws. If you cannot easily understand them in relation to your home and proposed business, speak with a zoning official or seek counsel from a local attorney familiar with the laws *and* their interpretation and application. We emphasize that because, in many communities, zoning laws have not kept pace with the reality that home-based businesses are one of the fastest-growing sectors of our increasingly entrepreneurial economy. In light of that, many communities have expanded the meanings of out-dated laws by giving them liberal interpretations.

(1) What To Do If You Meet Zoning Regulations
If your home business conforms to the existing regulations, then all you have to do is stay abreast of future zoning laws to make certain that any changes will not have a negative impact on your home-based business.

You might additionally do two other things, as well, so that you maintain friendly relations with your neighbors should you need their support in the future. (1) Join a neighborhood association, if there is one. This will keep you in touch with the mood of the neighborhood and reassure your neighbors that you are a cooperative, rather than an intrusive, presence in the neighborhood. (2) Seek out others who have home-based businesses and form a local "network" of entrepreneurs in circumstances similar to yours. Should adverse regulations affecting your business ever be proposed, you would have the advantage of an already existing support group sharing common interests in place.

(2) What To Do If You Don't Meet Zoning Regulations

If your home-based business does not conform to the existing regulation, then you have a problem — and several encouraging options.

You might check with an attorney who specializes in zoning law to receive his view of the regulation as it applies to you.

You might apply to the Zoning Board for a variance or exception to the exception. A creative attorney might well be successful in pursuing such an application on your behalf.

Or you may be able to change your business sufficiently to make your operation conform to the law. For example, if your local law outlaws businesses that employ people other than the owner at home, perhaps you can arrange for your employees to take work to their own homes.

The most difficult and dramatic option of all would be an attempt to get the law changed in its entirety. If your neighbors are sympathetic to your circumstances and there are other entrepreneurs facing similar difficulties because of the existing laws, you could well succeed — and become a local hero in the process!

Most opposition to a new home-based business comes from worried neighbors, concerned that your business might change the residential character of the neighborhood. If you can convince them otherwise, zoning officials will usually be responsive to your needs and permit you to proceed as planned.

"If you keep your premises neat and quiet and don't create traffic and parking problems," the SBA reports, "most neighborhoods will adopt a 'live and let live' attitude."

Selecting Your Form of Business Organization

You have three choices of business organization. Each has its advantages and disadvantages.

1. Sole proprietorship. This is the least costly and least complicated way of starting a business. A sole proprietorship can be organized almost instantly, so long as you meet local regulations (which we'll discuss later in this chapter).

Among its disadvantages are that you have unlimited personal liability with respect to the financial and legal obligations of the business and that (as the name suggests) the business will be entirely dependent on your good health and your good ideas for its growth and survival.

Nevertheless, because of its simplicity and directness, it is probably the most popular method of organizing a new business by an individual entrepreneur.

2. Partnership. If you will be joined in the founding of your business by one or more co-entrepreneurs, then forming a partnership is a possible form of organization for your venture. Legal fees for creating a partnership are usually more costly than those for creating a sole proprietorship but less costly than those for creating a corporation.

Among the disadvantages of a partnership are that it can be difficult to get rid of a bad partner, each general partner is bound by the decisions (and financial obligations) of every other general partner; and the death, withdrawal or bankruptcy of a partner can endanger the survival of the entire business.

Among its advantages are the additional capital a partner (or partners) can provide and the old adage that "two heads are better than one."

3. Corporation. Organizing a corporation is the most complicated and mostly costly of the three options. The greatest advantage of the corporate form of business organization is that its shareholders (its owners) have limited liability for the obligations of the firm.

However, the on-going accounting, legal and tax-reporting obligations of a corporation are considerably more demanding (and expensive and time-consuming) than those of a sole proprietorship or partnership.

There is a category of corporation which combines the protective feature of the traditional corporation (limited liability to its shareholders) while permitting the income (and losses) of the business to flow to you individually as if the corporation were a partnership or sole proprietorship.

This category of corporation is called the Subchapter S corporation. A "Sub-S" corporation (as it's typically called) must meet certain legal requirements as established by the Internal Revenue Service. Consult your attorney and accountant at the time you are organizing your business; they can advise you as to the possible benefits or disadvantages of this category or corporation as applied to your personal circumstances.

Meeting Regulations

When beginning a business, you will have to be in compliance with all applicable local, state and Federal regulations.

These will include such diverse details as filing a fictitious name certificate with the proper authorities (typically the County Clerk) if you are conducting a business under a name other than your own and acquiring the necessary tax and sales tax identification numbers and authorizations from your state's tax and revenue authorities. You will also have to apply for an Employer Identification Number (EIN) from the Internal Revenue Service; the EIN is a business' equivalent of an individual's Social Security Number.

There may be additional local regulations to fulfill; these can be determined by checking with a knowledgeable local attorney or accountant.

Specific businesses may be subject to special regulations. For example, if you are planning to start a catering business, you will have to make certain that you are complying with all applicable laws as administered by your local Health Department.

There is one legal problem peculiar to home-based businesses. Like many zoning laws, it is the product of old laws still in place in a world entirely different from the time when the laws were originally enacted. These are laws pertaining to certain businesses which *cannot* be performed in the home.

These laws were passed at a time when legislators were concerned about the exploitation of women and children in home-based "sweatshop" conditions. Sweatshops have essentially disappeared from the workplace but the laws are still in place. The laws of each state are different but some of the largest states still have strict "anti-homework" laws on their books. Again, you will have to make certain that your proposed business is exempt from these ancient regulations.

There is also a Federal equivalent of these state laws. It is called the "Fair Labor Standards Act" and must be evaluated by an attorney in relation to your proposed business.

The likelihood is that you will *not* be impacted by these long-standing laws. In the future, legislation proposed by a United States Senator entitled the "Freedom of the Workplace Act" might be enacted. Such passage would eliminate the Federal aspect of this problem.

Individual states, as well, are contemplating modern-day resolutions to these out-dated laws.

The early organizational requirements of the new home-based business can become complicated and cumbersome. They will, however, form the legal foundation of your business and will, therefore, have to be as complete and competent as possible.

During this period of organization, your best interests would be served by finding a first-rate attorney and a first-rate accountant. Each of them can help you negotiate this start-up process much more efficiently (and less stressfully) than you could on your own.

How can you find such professional counsel?

The most reliable approach is to seek recommendations from other home-based entrepreneurs who have already lived through this difficult period. If you trust their judgment, you will gain access to key professionals who will become invaluable allies as your business grows and prospers.

More and more attorneys and accountants are actively seeking "small business" clients — for two reasons. (1) This is the Age of the Entrepreneur and new businesses are being organized every day in every section of the country. (2) Many businesses which start small don't stay small — and that represents a "big business" opportunity for these professionals.

You are already in category (1). With any luck, you will soon find yourself in category (2)!

7

SETTING UP: WHAT YOU WILL NEED TO BEGIN

At the turn of the century, many small shop owners lived in apartments "over the store." Today, you are simply living at home. Tomorrow, you may be living *and* working at home. Thus, nearly 90 years later, you will be faced with the same problems which faced those small store owners: *Maintaining a clear separation and distinction between your working space and your living space.*

Depending on your particular personal circumstances, that can be a difficult distinction to achieve. No matter your circumstances, you *will* have to find a comfortable balance between these two suddenly proximate parts of your life.

Where Will You Work?

If you are living in a studio apartment in a city, your options will of necessity be severely limited. If you live on a family farm, you may have several "out" buildings to choose from as the location for your new home-based business.

The most typical circumstances are somewhere between these extremes.

Usually, the prospective home-based entrepreneur will be faced with one of six possibilities:

(1) Dividing an existing room which is currently in use.
(2) Using a spare room.
(3) Using the attic.
(4) Using the basement.
(5) Using the garage.
(6) Adding on a new room or wing.

Your own circumstances will determine your particular choice of location.

No matter which location you select, all locations have a number of fundamental elements in common: The location must be appropriate to your type of work. The location must be large enough to give you a sense of sufficient space. The location must be well lighted and heated (and, depending on the season or your part of the country, air-conditioned). Most importantly (unless you live in one of those one-room studio apartments we've already mentioned), you must be able to create a sense of separation between your at-home working environment and your at-home living environment.

You may want to invest in the services of an interior designer to help you to create the most efficient and comfortable possible use of the space available for your home office. In a way, you are too familiar with the space and may not be able to perceive all of the possibilities. An objective designer may pleasantly surprise you with a range of options which you didn't know existed within those familiar walls.

Privacy
You will want to have the ability to work alone undisturbed. Thus, you should be able to close off your working area, preferably to be able to lock it.

Quiet
You will want to work in a quiet environment and your family (if you do not live alone) will also want you to work in a quiet environment.

Thus, you should consider carpeting the space and covering the walls with materials which will absorb sound rather than amplify it.

Lighting
You will need a well-lighted environment in order to function efficiently — and safely. You may have to build in overhead lights and make such decisions as whether to install fluorescent lighting or incandescent lighting. Whichever you select, you will have to make certain that the lighting is evenly spread and not too harsh.

Fixtures and Outlets
You may never have paid attention to these items, but now they become important business installations.

You may have to accommodate a typewriter, a computer, a copier, a telephone answering machine and several desk lamps in a room which never had to accommodate more than a clock-radio before.

Thus, you may want to have an electrician survey the premises and make the necessary modifications. Most likely, your wiring and existing household electrical service will be able to carry the load of your new business equipment.

Security

You will want to be able to protect important business property and make your working premises as burglar-proof as possible.

Conventional locks and systems — both in your office and throughout your entire house — may be sufficient.

However, a security expert may be able to make additional recommendations, such as installing a suitable safe.

Fire Protection

Your at-home office will inevitably contain two ingredients which are notably flammable: Paper and wastebaskets.

Thus, you will want to have a fire extinguisher nearby and a smoke detector in place (if you don't already have one). You may also want to furnish your office with fire-resistant products.

Selecting Furniture

Do you have any idea what many home-based entrepreneurs consider to be the most important piece of furniture in their office?

The answer is *their personal chair!*

Apparently, once you have selected a comfortable chair, it's easy to put together the balance of your office.

On reflection, that makes a great deal of sense — although we will admit that we hadn't spent much time considering the matter.

The home-based entrepreneur will probably spend the majority of his time in his office chair — working, talking, thinking. So it is only logical that the selection of a comfortable, stress-reducing chair assumes priority on his furniture "wish list."

Once you've gotten past the seating, simply make certain that your furniture is able to withstand heavy use, is easy to clean and presents a professional appearance.

Work Flow

As we've suggested, your furniture should be comfortable. However, no matter how comfortable it is, it won't matter if the "flow" of your working space isn't equally comfortable.

Flow simply means creating a natural relationship between those portions of your office which you will be using with the greatest frequency. Thus, if you often pull items from a file, you should have a convenient filing cabinet within easy reach. Or, if you will be doing considerable typing, your machine should be reached without tripping across the office each time you have to use it.

Again, a designer who always works with these relationships may be able to help you to create the most efficient and comfortable flow permitted by the particular circumstances of your home office setting.

Telephones

Although you most likely already have a personal telephone at home, you will need a separate line for your business.

That separation will enable you to answer your business number in a consistent, confident manner — certain that it will not be an invitation to a party or a friendly neighbor calling to share some gossip in the middle of the work day.

Your business number will also have a separate listing in the phone book and, for expense-tracking purposes, you will have a clear picture of your business calling charges.

Answering Machine or Answering Service

Millions of them are in use, but we don't know of anyone who really likes to deal with a telephone answering machine when he is trying to reach a person.

On the other hand, answering machines are no longer a novelty and most of us have been conditioned to leave messages "at the sound of the tone" in spite of our dislike for the machines. From a budgeting point of view, an answering machine is a one-time expense; most machines can be reached from any "Touch-Tone" telephone in the world and, unless they're broken, they never miss a call.

Answering services do occasionally miss calls, and they require on-going monthly fees. However, they are answered by real people and can provide callers with specific instructions provided by you.

The choice, obviously, is personal and subjective: Neither decision is irreversible. Our experience has been that most new businesses install a machine, primarily because of its simplicity and low cost.

Typewriters

It used to be simple: A businessperson went out and bought a typewriter.

Today, it's no longer so simple. There are electric typewriters and electronic typewriters. There are word processors and computers with printers attached.

Whatever your selection, the most important universal quality of a letter-writing machine is the ability to produce crisp, high-quality, clear-resolution correspondence. Your customers should not be able to distinguish your correspondence from that of the president of the biggest bank in town!

Copiers

How did we ever live without them?

Today, there are many copiers on the market which are perfectly suited for small businesses. There are even hand-held portable models.

The cost has become so low that, for most new businesses, the question of leasing vs. buying is simply no longer an issue. They are affordable and, for the most part, reliable and inexpensive to maintain.

Computers

We cannot discuss the individual merits of specific brands or even the question of whether or not your particular business requires a computer.

We can remind you that the most critical long-term need, if you have a computer or are contemplating the purchase of one, is the quality and the capacity of your software, of the programs which you will employ. You will have to determine that they meet your current needs and have the ability to accommodate your future needs as you grow and your computer demands become more complicated.

Often, a reliable computer dealer can give you good advice in this regard. If you are uncertain about the quality or the objectivity of such information, you might consider hiring a computer consultant with expertise in your business.

Storage

You will have to maintain many records for extended periods of time, from tax returns to customer correspondence.

However, you do not have to share your "prime" space with these records. They can be stored in other areas of your house, from unused closets to open shelves in the garage. They will have to be protected so that children, pets and water leaks will not damage them. Thus, they should be stored in damage-resistant boxes and be kept out of harm's way insofar as your surroundings permit.

Stationery

Your letterheads, envelopes, bills and business cards are your "image" to the world. Thus, they should not be printed without careful thought.

For a home-based business in particular, stationery is its most visible presence — and it should present the business in the most favorable positive light.

A creative (often relatively inexpensive) graphic designer should be employed. Bond quality paper should be used and the entire "feel" of the stationery should be clear, confident and representative of the nature of your business.

Your business will most likely have additional office start-up requirements before opening for business. Virtually every business requires most of the items we are about to list. We call them **"Office Forget-Me-Nots:"**

Tape
Pens and pencils
Stapler and staples
File folders
Manila envelopes
Postage stamps
Rubber stamps
Rubber bands
Typewriter ribbons
Pocket calculator
Petty cash

8

MAKING IT SAFE: FROM INSURANCE TO DOGS TO VISITORS

This chapter is about insurance — and about "business-proofing" your house once you begin to work at home.

You may know where your children drop their toys and where your dog hides his bones, but visitors to your premises will not have such knowledge — and if they trip and break their leg, they are not going to sue your children or your dog. They are going to look to you for compensation.

We have already spoken about giving your office space a "professional look." Now we are talking about making it safe, as well. Remove any possible perils that may exist, so that chances for an accident on your property are minimized. You may be familiar with the old saw that "most accidents happen at home." Now your home and office are one and the same — so you will have to be twice as safety-conscious!

In all likelihood, whether you own or rent your home or apartment, you have some existing homeowner's insurance in place. Now that your premises will be used for commercial purposes, the terms of your present policies are probably inadequate — and, in some instances, may deny you protection all together because you have altered the use of your property.

Your insurance broker will be able to advise you about the terms of your specific policy and about what you must do to protect your home and business now that they share the same location.

You will be concerned with three general classes of insurance.

(1) Coverages that are essential for most businesses.

(2) Coverages that are desirable for many businesses but not absolutely necessary.

(3) Coverages for employee benefits.

Essential Coverages

Four kinds of insurance are essential: fire insurance, liability insurance, automobile insurance, and worker's compensation insurance.

Fire Insurance

Other perils — such as explosion, vandalism and malicious mischief — can be added to your basic fire insurance at relatively small additional cost. Usually, your best buy will be an "all-risk" policy which affords comprehensive coverage.

If you expect to collect the full amount of your loss, you will have to agree to the so-called "coinsurance clause" in your policy. This clause states that you must carry insurance equal to 80 or 90 percent of the value of your insured property. If you carry less than this, you cannot collect the full amount of your loss, even if the loss is small.

Liability Insurance

Legal liability limits of $1 million are no longer considered high or unreasonable even for a small business.

Most liability policies, in addition to bodily injuries, may now cover personal injuries — such as libel and slander — if these are specifically insured.

Obviously, your liability coverage will cover your premises — so that if anyone sustains an injury in your home, you are protected against such loss.

You will probably be spending a great deal of your time out of your home office — visiting clients, etc. Your liability coverage should be extended to insure you under those circumstances, as well.

Automobile Insurance

The higher you are willing to make your deductible — the amount of money which you will pay yourself in the event of an accident — the lower your premium. $250 and $500 are common deductibles, but you can increase that to $1000 or more — and decrease your premium.

When an employee or subcontractor uses a car on your behalf, you can be legally liable even though you don't own the car or truck. Make certain that you are covered for such a possibility.

Worker's Compensation

If you are the only employee of your business, you do not require Worker's Compensation coverage.

Federal and common law requires that an employer (1) provide employees a safe place to work, (2) hire competent fellow employees, (3) provide safe tools, and (4) warn employees of an existing danger.

If an employer fails to provide the above, the employer is liable for damage suits brought by an employee and possible fines or prosecution.

Worker's compensation is under the jurisdiction of the individual states, and thus benefits will vary from state to state. In nearly all states, you are now legally required to cover your workers under Worker's Compensation.

Desirable Coverages

Some types of insurance coverage, while not absolutely essential, will add greatly to the security of your business. These coverages include business interruption insurance, crime insurance, product liability insurance and so-called "floater" coverage.

Business Interruption Insurance
You can purchase insurance to cover fixed expenses that would continue if a fire shut down your business — such as salaries to key employees, taxes, interest, depreciation, and utilities — as well as the profits you would lose.

You can also get coverage for the extra expenses you suffer if an insured peril, while not actually closing your business down, seriously disrupts it.

Crime Insurance
A comprehensive crime policy written just for small business owners is available. In addition to burglary and robbery, it covers other types of loss by theft, destruction and disappearance of money and securities. It also covers thefts by your employees.

Product and Service Liability Insurance
If you are in a manufacturing business, you will want to have coverage against any prospective damage caused by a

malfunctioning of your products.

If you are in a service business, you will want to consider "errors and omissions" insurance, which can be compared to malpractice insurance in terms of its protection to the insured (you).

Both of these coverages are within the broad definition of "commercial liability insurance." It is a category which does not lend itself to generalizations because every separate policy is written to meet the specific needs of your particular business, product or service.

"Floater" Coverage

This is really an extension of your basic fire insurance, which sets limits on the loss of personal property.

By specifying individual possessions — from computers to works of art — you can cover important, expensive items for full value.

Every additional item carries a separate premium, but the extended coverage will provide you with additional peace of mind.

Employee Benefit Coverages

If you are the only employee, you will be most concerned with disability and retirement insurance. If you have additional employees, group health and life insurance become a consideration. And if you have partners or employees crucial to the operation of your business, you may want to purchase keyman insurance.

Group Health Insurance

Group health insurance costs much less and provides more generous benefits for the worker than individual contracts would. If you pay the entire cost, individual employees cannot be dropped from a group unless the entire group policy is cancelled.

Group Life Insurance

If you pay group insurance premiums and cover all employees up to $50,000, the cost to you is deductible for Federal income tax purposes and yet the value of the benefits is not taxable income to your employees.

Disability Insurance

Group disability insurance coverage is not as common as group health and life coverage. However, it is coverage you should seriously consider on your own behalf. Disability is a serious threat to everyone, and an especially serious threat to the entrepreneur. We could make the argument that for the self-employed entrepreneur who depends on his own continued good health to prosper, disability insurance should be moved into the "Essential Coverages" category.

Key-Man Insurance

One of the most serious setbacks that can come to a small company is the loss of a key employee. Your key employees can be insured with life insurance owned by and payable to the company.

The premiums are *not* a deductible business expense, but the proceeds of a key man policy are not subject to income tax.

Retirement Income

Being self-employed, you can get an income tax deduction for funds used for retirement for you and your employees through plans of insurance or annuities approved for use under the Employees Retirement Income Security Act of 1974 (ERISA).

These plans, however, will require the counsel of your accountant and attorney in addition to your insurance agent.

Insurance is a complex and detailed subject and this chapter is intended simply as a checklist for home business owners. You will need the assistance of a professionally qualified agent, broker or consultant to explain the options, recommend the right coverage, and help you avoid financial loss.

9

THE TAX ASPECTS OF YOUR HOME-BASED BUSINESS

Tax laws relating to home-based businesses have historically been subject to constant changes and challenges. *The Tax Reform Act of 1986,* despite publicity proclaiming its simplicity, has *not* simplified tax matters as they relate to home-based entrepreneurs.

The material in this chapter is based on the Act and pertains mainly to *full-time at-home entrepreneurs.* (The requirements for part-time at-home entrepreneurs and employees who work at home on behalf of their employers, if they are of importance to you, should be discussed and evaluated with an accountant, a tax attorney or the IRS.)

What The IRS Requires
In Order To Claim
A Home Office Deduction

To claim a home office deduction which meets the IRS requirements, you must be able to establish that your home office is used *both exclusively and regularly* for business purposes.

That requirement is absolute and must be met by every taxpayer who takes the home office deduction. Additionally, you must meet *at least one* of these three tests:

(1) Your home office is your principal place of business.

(2) Your home office is a place where you *regularly* meet customers, clients or patients.

(3) Your home office is a separate structure not attached to your home.

There are two specific exceptions to the *exclusive use* test. One applies to day care facilities for children, adults over 65 or physically or mentally impaired people. The other — which directly affects many home-based entrepreneurs — applies to those portions of the home which are used on a regular basis to store inventory and goods which are sold at retail or wholesale in a trade or business.

To deduct expenses in connection with storage space, you have to meet *each* of these five tests:

(1) The inventory must be stored for use in your trade or business.

(2) Your trade or business must be the selling of such inventory at either wholesale or retail.

(3) Your home must be the sole fixed location of that trade or business.

(4) The storage space must be suitable for the purpose and be a separately identifiable part of your home.

(5) The storage space must be used on a regular basis.

Thus, for example, a home-based mail order entrepreneur would have *two* available deductions: One for his home office and another for his home storage space.

If You Meet The IRS Requirements, How Much Can You Deduct?

We will talk about the home office deduction, but the same rules apply to the home storage space deduction.

If, for example, you live in a 2000-square-foot house, and your office (which meets all of the IRS requirements) is 10 x 20 (200-square-feet), your home office constitutes 10% of your entire house.

Thus, you can deduct 10% of all expenses which relate to the *entire* house.

As common examples, you can deduct 10% of all utility costs, 10% of garbage collection costs, 10% of water costs, etc.

These are considered to be *indirect* expenses — and can only be deducted in proportion to the size of your office space as divided by the size of the entire house.

There are some *direct* expenses which can be deducted in their entirety. Examples would be the cost of painting your office space or the cost of repairing a leak in your office — so long as the expense only benefits your home office space rather than any other (non-business) part of the house.

Deducting Depreciation

Depreciation is a very complicated concept. In its simplest form, it is the allocation of the cost of an asset over a certain period of time. That period is traditionally considered, by the IRS, to be "its useful life." The calculation of that depreciation is different for different assets; and each application of depreciation must be determined on a case-by-case basis together with the appropriate tax experts.

However, *The Tax Reform Act of 1986* is very specific about deducting depreciation for a home office located in a house *purchased or placed in service after December 31, 1986.* (For deductions relating to houses purchased or placed in service *before* that date, you must consult with your accountant or attorney.)

For a house purchased or placed in service after the effective date above, the allowable depreciation is as follows:

The cost of the house divided by 31.5 years.

Say your house cost $90,000. If you divide $90,000 by 31.5, you arrive at $2857.14 per year for 31.5 years.

If your home office constitutes 10% of your house, you are entitled to deduct 10% of the $2857.14 — *or $285.71 per year.*

Note: If, in the future, you sell your house *during a year in which you have taken the deduction for depreciation,* the amount of that year's depreciation deduction and your depreciation deductions for earlier years are subject to what the IRS call *recapture.* In such an event, you will have to determine your tax liability in consultation with your attorney or accountant.

Deducting The Cost of Computers And Other Business Furnishings

Again, the rules are too complex for easy generalizations applicable to all circumstances. However, three generalizations *can* be made.

(1) If your home office computer is used for business purposes at least 50% of the time, it is subject to depreciation over 5 years.

(2) Most other business equipment and furnishings are subject to depreciation over 7 years.

(3) *The Tax Reform Act of 1986* provides you with an election: You may elect to deduct up to $10,000 of the purchase price of depreciable business property during the first year it is placed in service. Thus, you may "expense" rather than depreciate the cost of such equipment (up to $10,000) — subject to certain limitations which can be explained to you by a knowledgeable tax attorney or accountant.

Depreciating A Car
Used At Least 50% For Business

Depreciation for automobiles purchased or placed in service after December 31, 1986 is subject to complicated computations requiring the services of an accountant or attorney.

However, we can report the *maximum* amount of depreciation allowable for a car placed in service or purchased after that effective date:

Year 1: You can depreciate a maximum of $2,560.
Year 2: You can depreciate a maximum of $4,100.
Year 3: You can depreciate a maximum of $2,450.
Thereafter: You can depreciate a maximum of $1,475.

Health Insurance

For the years 1987, 1988 and 1989, a self-employed person can deduct 25% of the premiums which he paid for health insurance.

This deduction, which is a new benefit for the self-employed, is subject to one caveat: If you have employees, you must make the same insurance coverage you maintain for yourself available to them. If you do not, you cannot take the deduction.

How You Can Deduct Sales Tax

The sales tax deduction was one of the most publicized "victims" of *The Tax Reform Act of 1986.*

Although sales tax is no longer deductible as an itemized deduction, *it can be included as part of the original cost of an asset which may be depreciated for business use.* Thus, over time, under this scenario, the home-based entrepreneur can indirectly deduct the sales tax attached to that item.

This chapter is shorter than some single paragraphs in the Internal Revenue Code! Thus, obviously, it is intended to do nothing more than give you a basic understanding of some of the main tax benefits available to home-based, self-employed taxpayers.

The Tax Reform Act of 1986 may be modified by legislation, and it will certainly be subject to interpretation by the courts and by the IRS itself.

Thus, be certain to consult with your attorney and accountant before making any business judgments which may affect your personal tax status and the tax status of your home-based business.

10

THE RECORDS YOU MUST MAINTAIN FOR YOUR HOME-BASED BUSINESS

It is well established that the burden of proof to substantiate income and expenses falls on the taxpayer, not the tax collector. Yet, the tax collector — the Internal Revenue Service — has not established *how* these records should be created and maintained. Thus, the burden of proof is yours — and the freedom to organize the most useful record-keeping system you can devise is yours, as well.

What Your Records Must Be Able To Tell You At A Glance

Your home-based business (every business, in fact) should be able to derive three critical pieces of data from its records at any time:

(1) **How much cash you owe.**

(2) **How much cash you are due.**

(3) **How much cash you have on hand.**

To Track These Three Facts, You Will Need To Maintain Five Basic Journals

(1) **Check Register:** This should record each check you disburse, the date of the disbursement, the number of the check, to whom it was made out (the payee), the amount of money disbursed, and for what purposed the payment was made.

(2) **Cash Receipts:** This should show the amount of money received, from whom, and for what.

(3) **Sales Journal:** This should record each business transaction, the date of the transaction, for whom it was performed and the amount of the invoice (including sales tax, if applicable).

(4) **Voucher Register:** This is a record of bills, money owed, the date of the bill, to whom it is owed, the amount, and the service performed or the product sold.

(5) **General Journal:** This is a means of adjusting some entries in the other four journals, a record-keeping technique your accountant will explain to you when he helps you to set up your business record-keeping system.

What Kind of Record-Keeping System Should You Use?

It depends on the nature of your business, and can best be

determined after an analysis of your particular business' needs together with your accountant.

Sometimes, a record-keeping system (at least at the beginning) can be incredibly simple, as simple as setting up different envelopes for different purposes: *An expense envelope, an income envelope, a bills outstanding envelope, etc.* Such a primitive method usually becomes cumbersome, despite its simplicity, and has to be replaced by a less casual system.

Many home business owners, who own a computer, employ one of the many useful (and increasingly inexpensive) computer programs designed to help a business keep track of its income and expenses. These programs can serve many other business purposes, as well, and can give a small business a level of record-keeping sophistication which was once only available to large companies.

Finding the best programs — or software — can be a challenging task. You will want to buy programs which can expand as your business activities expand — and ones which will not quickly become obsolete. Because the importance, availability and usefulness of computer software has exploded in recent years, you may find assistance in regard to record-keeping and money-management programs from sources you would not ordinarily consider. Some of the most current, state-of-the-art programs are being developed (and sold) by major accounting firms and local banks.

Keeping Track of "Hidden" Expenses

Every business suffers from "hidden" expenses which the small business owner often forgets to record — but which can make a considerable difference to your "bottom line."

They are different for each business, but these examples will give you a sense of the possibilities.

Every business should make provisions for bounced checks, which are usually returned because of "insufficient funds."

If you have a mail order (or any other retail) business, you must be certain to make a provision for returns, merchandise returned by customers. A common error is to consider such merchandise "sold" and then to fail to make the accounting adjustment reversing that record of sale when it is returned.

If you are in a service business, you should compare the amount of time you estimated a project would take to the amount of time it actually did take. Time *is* money, especially for the self-employed home-based business owner, and if your estimates are often wrong, you will have a "hidden" expense which will not remain in hiding for long!

It is difficult to make generalities, but it is not difficult to suggest that every business has such pitfalls, such "hidden" expenses, and that keeping track of them — and making adjustments once you have established what they are *really* costing you in time and money — is a record-keeping priority.

Miscellaneous Records

We are simply going to list three of the records most common to a broad variety of businesses.

Advertising Expenses
In this category, you should include everything from the cost of a Yellow Pages ad to the cost of the phone calls which you made soliciting new business. It is not a bad idea to keep

a simultaneous record of what each advertising expenditure produced in new revenue.

Customer Records
Your business is built on satisfied customers, and the more you know about each of them, the better your chances for repeat business. Some records in this category are obvious, e.g., keeping a record of customers' sizes if you are in the clothing business. Others are not quite so obvious, e.g., keeping track of customers' favorite waiters if you are in the catering business.

The more you know about your customers, the better you will be able to serve them — and sell them!

Telephone Record-Checking
The telephone can be insidious. You can find yourself using it when you're not even aware of it!

Not only can misuse of the phone cost you time, it can cost you surprisingly large sums of money. Be sure that you have not been charged for calls or information requests you didn't make, equipment you didn't rent or services which were not provided. Many professionals "log" each of their calls; it is not a bad idea for every business to do that occasionally.

The Benefits of Keeping Good Records

Every business *has* to maintain records, so they might as well carry a number of benefits with them — and these are three of the best benefits which will accrue to you as the product of good record-keeping:

(1) Your accounting bills will be reduced. Accountants typically bill for the hours they work on your business. If they can locate the information they need quickly and efficiently, your bills for accounting services can be dramatically lowered.

(2) **You won't worry about the IRS.** The IRS may not tell you how to keep your records, but they certainly expect you to produce complete and accurate records in case they have a question. Good records are a taxpayer's strongest defense.

(3) **You'll sleep better — for two reasons.** The first reason is (2) above, and the second reason is that you will always be confident that your record-keeping system can provide you with the factual, bottom-line information you need to make better — and more profitable — business decisions.

11

HOW TO MAKE YOUR HOME-BASED BUSINESS CREDIT-WORTHY

The greatest single reason for business failure is lack of sufficient funding. This book is not designed to help you raise money, but it is designed to help you manage your business — and your business' money.

Therefore, the best advice we can give you is that if you can establish cordial and productive relationships with three groups of people, your money management worries can be significantly reduced. These groups are:

(1) **Your local banks.**

(2) **Your suppliers.**

(3) **Your customers.**

Your Local Bank

There is some truth to the saying that "banks will only lend you money when you *don't* need it." Thus, it makes sense to introduce yourself to your banker of choice at a time when you don't want anything from him.

Chances are that you already have a personal banking relationship with a bank in your town. If you have been a steady customer, perhaps one who has taken and repaid some loans promptly, then you have an advantage when you are seeking to extend that personal relationship to a business relationship.

A banker familiar with you will most likely welcome you, and give you helpful advice with respect to opening and maintaining a business checking account at his institution. He may even offer you "preferred" fees because of your previous relationship with the bank. He will appreciate an explanation from you about your new business and be flattered by your offer to keep him updated on new business developments.

In turn, you can be candid asking about such matters as banking fees, special services and future loan requests. If you sense a positive, mutually supportive attitude, you can probably stop looking for a business banker elsewhere.

If, on the other hand, you are in the position of beginning a relationship with a new bank, then an introduction (from a local businessperson or accountant or attorney) will give you greater credibility at the institution. A new banker — every banker, really — will appreciate current information about your business so that by the time you approach him for a loan, he will already "know" your business and be more inclined to approve a loan to a familiar face.

Your Suppliers

In your own business, you will be concerned about being paid for services performed and merchandise produced. So you can appreciate the concern a supplier might initially have about a new business customer — even if that customer is you.

Therefore, you will have to put yourself in his place. If he understands and believes your business plan, and believes you to be reliable and responsible, he may well offer you some credit. It may not be for the cost of an entire order, but even a partial deferral of payment due is helpful to a new business.

Suppliers are often prepared to act (in effect) as bankers, lending you their product or service rather than money. They expect you to live up to your understanding with them — and the consequences can be damaging to your future business-credit prospects if you don't.

As we note in Chapter 13, word-of-mouth can be a very helpful marketing technique — if it is favorable to you, your product or service. Conversely, word-of-mouth can be damaging if the words are of anger, disappointment or distrust. Therefore, be certain to honor and protect your relationships with your suppliers.

Your Customers

Customers might appear to be an unlikely source of credit — and they are not really credit sources in the traditional sense. They are more accurately sources of accelerated cash flow — putting money in your hands sooner.

Often, a new home-based business owner is so grateful for the order, for the customer's business, that he is afraid to ask "for anything" from the customer.

We are suggesting that you ask for something that is yours — or eventually will be yours — the money you will be receiving for performing a service or delivering a product. To a new business especially, *now* is the most important three-letter word in the dictionary.

You will be pleasantly surprised to discover that most of your customers will easily agree to give you early or partial payments. They will respond to your need, and appreciate your self-confidence and your confidence in them.

This type of accommodation is less likely to occur in a retail business, and is most likely to be available to home-based service businesspeople.

To each of these groups — the banks, your suppliers and your customers — the most important consideration in extending you credit is your reputation and your business conduct.

If you meet your obligations timely; report any unforseen problems to them without hesitation, and generally "take care of business" as promised, you will be in the most desirable category of all: *A business they want to do business with.*

12

HOW TO BUDGET AND MANAGE YOUR TIME WHEN WORKING AT HOME

Each of us, from time to time, puts off doing something "until later."

It is a trap which a home-based businessperson can easily — and quite understandably — fall into.

It is a trap which you, as a home-based businessperson, must avoid at all cost — because the cost can be as high as this: Your home-based business will fail because you replace productivity with procrastination!

Regular Business Hours

When you worked in an office or at a plant, you were expected to report to work at a regular, established time each day.

You must expect no less of yourself when you are working at home.

You must establish — and adhere to — regular business hours.

This pattern will remind you each day that, at least during business hours, your home *is* your office, the place where you have elected to conduct your business. You must conduct your business in a business-like manner: *That productive attitude begins by maintaining regular business hours.*

Getting Dressed

We will add an important proviso here, one that is not nearly as funny as it sounds: *Get dressed!*

Occasionally, a home business owner may have the tendency to "roll out of bed" into his office, without changing clothes.

This is a terrible idea, because it will dilute your image of yourself as a productive businessperson.

As we've already noted, the ability to dress casually is one of the home business owner's enjoyable "perks." Be careful not to extend that sense of casualness to not dressing at all!

First, Set Goals

Long-range planning may be a desirable business school and corporate concept but it doesn't often work for the home business owner.

We suggest that you establish four reasonable categories of goals, of your reasonable business objectives:

    (1) **What has to be done today.**

    (2) **What has to be done tomorrow.**

    (3) **What has to be done next week.**

    (4) **What has to be done next month.**

Next, Set Your Priorities

Not every goal or objective is equal. Therefore, you will have to establish some priorities.

If you are listing your goals on paper, highlight your priorities with a transparent marker so that they stand out from your less pressing tasks.

Now, Keep Your Own Word

Your good intentions now have to be converted into action.

You must keep track of your objectives and priorities; they should be acted upon and reviewed during every working day. Two techniques should help you achieve them.

(1) "Bunching"

Group similar tasks together. For example:

● Make all of your phone calls during a time set aside only for that task.

● Schedule out-of-office appointments with proximity so that you can accomplish a series of visits on a single trip.

● Write or dictate all of your correspondence at the same time.

● Set aside a specific time for specific tasks, *e.g.,* billing. This will save you time and mis-appropriation of energy.

"Bunching" will enable you to concentrate your energies on a related group of functions, increasing your productivity and safeguarding against deferring a given series of tasks "until later."

(2) Become Your Own Management Consultant

Surprise — and test — yourself. Every so often, keep a very accurate daily log, or diary, of your activities. *Do not omit anything you do during the day — including drinking a cup of coffee, playing with the dog or doodling on your scratch pad.*

Then, at day's end, carefully review your activities.

Chances are your log will surprise you — and encourage you to change (for the better) many aspects of the way you work. This is a wonderfully effective method of reviewing — and improving — your time-management habits.

One of the most useful advantages of having a home office is the elimination of that dreaded daily marathon known as *the commute.*

The time you formerly spent traveling to and from work — all of your working time, in fact — can be used to great advantage because of the proximity of your home and office.

All you have to do is make certain to use it!

HOW TO MARKET YOUR HOME-BASED BUSINESS

The purpose of marketing is simple: *To make as many of your likely customers as possible aware of your business and the service or products it sells.*

First, You Have To Know Your Market

Your general understanding of your market must be converted into a much more specific definition of your market so that you can target your prospects.

Thus, simply saying, "I'm in advertising" isn't sufficient.

If, in fact, you are in advertising, you have to begin to make some realistic assumptions: The biggest companies in town are most likely not looking for one-person advertising agencies. The local offices of national or international organizations are also most likely not looking for one-person advertising agencies (or any agencies at all; marketing may be directed from their headquarters which are elsewhere).

There are, however, lots of smaller companies, new businesses and professional people who *are* in the market for an advertising professional who will not consider their account to be unimportant.

Once you've established the broader outlines of your market, you can refine them down to even more specific targets.

For example, if you had developed a good reputation as an advertising professional with special expertise in the retail business before setting out on your own, it would make sense to seek the type of clients who could best use that skill.

Whatever your business, the first rule of marketing is: *Know your market.*

Advertising Can Be Helpful

Advertising means that you will pay someone — a newspaper, a television station, a publisher of telephone directories — to deliver the message that you are in business.

There are several problems with relying on advertising to build a new business.

(1) You probably don't have enough money to advertise as often as you would like — and repetition is an important attribute of a successful advertising campaign.

(2) You will be "wasting" a lot of money. That portion of an audience not considered likely to purchase your product or service is considered to be "waste." Most advertising media will reach many readers or listeners who have no interest in your product or service — and yet you are paying to reach them.

(3) Advertising is not as effective as promotion.

Promotion Is More Helpful

Whereas you will have to pay for advertising, promotion will not cost you anything — directly. Indirectly, the cost of promotion will include all of the expenses incurred in reaching those people who can promote you, your product or your service.

These would include editors, columnists, television producers and radio talk show hosts.

If you or your product or service are sufficiently unique or interesting to warrant coverage by a newspaper, magazine, radio or television station, you will have a distinct marketing advantage.

Studies indicate that consumers regard "editorial" coverage with less skepticism and more enthusiasm than "advertising" material.

Thus, if you can successfully promote yourself and your product or service, you will have achieved significant credibility while saving considerable advertising expense.

Promotion is the most promising marketing medium for the new, start-up, home-based business.

Word-of-Mouth Is Best of All

Satisfied customers are the most valuable asset of any business. If you are able to satisfy your customers, they will build your reputation faster than any carefully planned advertising and promotion program.

Money can't buy happiness — or two of the three marketing elements we have just presented. Thus, having a small advertising budget (or no budget at all) should not discourage you from marketing your new business. Creative promotion and satisfied customers can be a new business' most effective marketing tools.

14

WHEN TO THINK ABOUT MAKING THE MOVE OUT OF YOUR HOME

There may come a time when you wake up one morning, look around your house — which, of course, is also your office and the "world headquarters" of your business — and decide that you have to move your business out of the house.

You may have simply run out of space, your business may have grown too large to still "fit" in the house or the boundaries between the business and non-business portions of your house may have become so blurred that there is no longer any separation between the two.

Should that happen to you, you will have three options available to you.

You Can Move The Business Out Of The House

At first, when you made the decision to run your business

out of your home, you had to make all of the adjustments of which we have spoken throughout this book.

Now, however, you are completely adjusted and totally comfortable (maybe even spoiled!) with your home office environment — and the prospect of having to work in a "regular" office is making you uneasy.

Of course, you may have no other option available to you — and therefore you will have to re-locate your home office out of the house.

Even in large cities, there are smaller office buildings or "brownstones" available for rent, so that such a move might not be as traumatic as you might fear. But that approach doesn't appeal to you. What can you do?

You Can Move Part of Your Business Out of The House

Professionals have long divided parts of their practices between two or more locations. A psychiatrist, for instance, might see his individual patients at home and conduct his group therapy sessions at another location.

Perhaps you can move a portion of the business out of the house while maintaining other functions in place. If you need space for a showroom or "back office" space for computer operations which you can no longer accommodate at home, you might be able to add a second location without giving up your home office space entirely.

You Can Move To A Bigger House

Many home office entrepreneurs refuse to return to their

former lifestyle. They love having their home and office under the same roof and would never consider "going back" to the way it was.

For these entrepreneurs, there is only one solution: *Moving to a bigger house!*

15

MEET THE SBA — INCLUDING A COMPLETE LIST OF ALL U.S. SMALL BUSINESS ADMINISTRATION FIELD OFFICES

There is an agency of the Federal government whose mission is made-to-order for the home-based entrepreneur, as well as every other self-employed independent businessperson. That agency is the U.S. Small Business Administration, commonly called the SBA.

The SBA's own description of its main job is remarkably direct: *"The mission of SBA, simply put, is to help people get into business and stay in business."*

Who Will The SBA Assist?

The SBA was created by Congress in 1953 "to assist, counsel and champion the millions of American small businesses which are the backbone of this country's competitive free-enterprise economy."

What Is A Small Business?

The SBA "generally defines a small business as one which is independently owned and operated and is not dominant in its field. To be eligible for SBA loans and other assistance, a business must meet a size standard set by the Agency. Specific size standard information is available through any SBA office around the country."

What Services Does The SBA Offer Small Businesses?

Among the many services and programs which the SBA offers small businesses are these:

Financial Assistance: The SBA offers a variety of loan programs to eligible small businesses "which cannot borrow on reasonable terms from conventional lenders without government help."

Management Assistance: The SBA offers free individual counseling, courses, conferences, workshops, problem clinics, and a wide range of publications.

Special Assistance to Women, Veterans and Minorities: These groups are eligible for all SBA programs but the Agency has targeted them for special attention to help bring them into the mainstream of the American entrepreneurial economy.

Procurement Assistance: Each year, the Federal government contracts with private companies for billions of dolars in goods and services. The SBA "helps small business obtain a fair share of this government business."

There is no charge for any SBA service. Its services are invaluable to the small businessperson. Therefore, we are publishing the complete list of SBA Field Offices:

List of SBA Field Offices

Alabama
908 South 20th Street
Birmingham, Alabama 35256
205/254-1344

Alaska
Federal Building
701 C Street, Box 67
Anchorage, Alaska 99513
907/271-4022

Box 14
101 12th Avenue
Fairbanks, Alaska 99701
907/456-0211

Arizona
3030 North Central Avenue
Suite 1201
Phoenix, Arizona 85012
602/241-2206

301 West Congress Street
Federal Building, Box 33
Tucson, Arizona 85701
602/792-6715

Arkansas
320 West Capitol Avenue
Suite 601
Little Rock, Arkansas 72201
501/378-5871

California
2202 Monterey Street
Fresno, California 93721
209/487-5791

660 J Street, Suite 215
Sacramento, California
95814
916/440-2956

880 Front Street,
Room 4-S-29
San Diego, California 92188
714/293-5444

450 Golden Gate Avenue
Box 36044
San Francisco, California
94102
415/556-7487

211 Main Street, 4th Floor
San Francisco, California
94105
415/974-0594

350 South Figueroa Street
Sixth Floor
Los Angeles, California
90071
213/688-2956

Fidelity Federal Building
2700 North Main Street
Suite 400
Santa Ana, California 92701
714/836-2494

111 West St. John Street
Room 424
San Jose, California 95113
408/291-7584

Colorado
Executive Tower Building
1405 Curtis Street
22nd Floor
Denver, Colorado
80202-2395
303/844-5441

721 19th Street
Room 420
Denver, Colorado
80202-2599
303/844-3984

Connecticut
One Hartford Square West
Hartford, Connecticut 06106
203/240-4700

Delaware
844 King Street
Room 5207
Lockbox 16
Wilmington, Delaware 19801
302/573-6294

District of Columbia
1111 18th St., N.W.
Sixth Floor
Washington, D.C. 20036
202/634-1818

Florida
400 West Bay Street
Room 261
P.O. Box 35067
Jacksonville, Florida 32202
904/791-3782

2222 Ponce De Leon Blvd.
5th Floor
Coral Gables, Florida 33134
305/350-5521

700 Twiggs Street
Suite 607
Tampa, Florida 33602
813/228-2594

3500 45th Street
Suite 6
West Palm Beach, Florida
33407
305/689-2223

Georgia
Federal Building - Room 225
52 North Main Street
Statesboro, Georgia 30458
912/489-8719

1375 Peachtree Street, N.E.
5th Floor
Atlanta, Georgia 30367
404/881-4948

1720 Peachtree Road, N.W.
6th Floor
Atlanta, Georgia 30309
404/881-4325

Guam
Pacific News Building
Room 508
238 O'Hara Street
Agana, Guam 96910
671/472-7277

Hawaii
300 Ala Moana
Room 2213
P.O. Box 50207
Honolulu, Hawaii 96850
808/546-8950

Idaho
1020 Main Street
2nd Floor
Boise, Idaho 83702
208/334-1096

Illinois
230 South Dearborn Street
Room 510
Chicago, Illinois 60604
312/353-4542

219 South Dearborn Street
Room 437
Chicago, Illinois 60604
312/353-4528

Washington Building
Four North Old State
Capitol Plaza
Springfield, Illinois 62701
217/492-4416

Indiana
River Glen Office Plaza
Suite 160
South Bend, Indiana 46601
219/236-8361

New Federal Building
5th Floor
575 North Pennsylvania St.
Indianapolis, Indiana
46204-1584
317/269-7278

Iowa
210 Walnut Street
Des Moines, Iowa 50309
515/284-4567

373 Collins Road, N.E.
Cedar Rapids, Iowa 52402
319/399-2571

Kansas
Main Place Building
110 East Waterman Street
Wichita, Kansas 67202
316/269-6273

Kentucky
Federal Office Building
P.O. Box 3517 Room 188
Louisville, Kentucky 40201
502/582-5971

Louisiana
Ford-Fisk Building
1661 Canal Street
2nd Floor
New Orleans, Louisiana
70112
504/589-6685

500 Fannin Street
Federal Bldg. & Courthouse
Room 5 B04
Shreveport, Louisiana 71101
318/226-5196

Maine
40 Western Avenue
Room 512
Augusta, Maine 04330
207/622-8378

Maryland
8600 LaSalle Road
Room 630
Towson, Maryland 21204
301/962-2233

Massachusetts
60 Batterymarch Street
10th Floor
Boston, Massachusetts 02110
617/223-1005

150 Causeway Street
10th Floor
Boston, Massachusetts 02114
617/223-7991

Federal Bldg. & Courthouse
1550 Main Street, Room 212
Springfield, Massachusetts
01103
413/785-0268

Michigan
477 Michigan Avenue
McNamara Building
Room 515
Detroit, Michigan 48226
313/226-6075

220 West Washington Street
Suite 310
Marquette, Michigan 49885
906/225-1108

Minnesota
610-C Butler Square
100 North 6th Street
Minneapolis, Minnesota
55403
612/349-3574

Mississippi
Gulf National Life
Insurance Building
111 Fred Haise Boulevard
2nd Floor
Biloxi, Mississippi 39530
601/435-3676

100 West Capitol Street
Federal Building
Suite 322
Jackson, Mississippi 39269
601/960-4371-4372

Missouri
911 Walnut Street
13th Floor
Kansas City, Missouri 64106
816/374-3316

1103 Grand Avenue
6th Floor
Kansas City, Missouri 64106
816/374-5557

815 Olive Street
Room 242
St. Louis, Missouri 63101
314/425-6600

339 Broadway
Room 140
Cape Girardeau, Missouri
63701
314/335-6039

309 North Jefferson
Springfield, Missouri 65806
417/864-7670

Montana
301 South Park Avenue
Room 528, Drawer 10054
Helena, Montana 59626
406/449-5381

Billings Post-of-Duty
Post Office Building
Room 216
2601 First Avenue North
Billings, Montana 59101
406/657-6047

Nebraska
Empire State Building
19th & Farnam Streets
Omaha, Nebraska 68102
402/221-4691

Nevada
Box 7527—Downtown Sta.
301 East Stewart
Las Vegas, Nevada 89101
702/385-6611

P.O. Box 3216
50 South Virginia Street
Room 308
Reno, Nevada 89505
702/784-5268

New Hampshire
55 Pleasant Street
Concord, New Hampshire
03301
603/224-4724

New Jersey
1800 East Davis Street
Camden, New Jersey 08104
609/757-5183

60 Park Place, 4th Floor
Newark, New Jersey 07102
201/645-3683

New Mexico
Patio Plaza Building
5000 Marble Avenue, N.E.
Albuquerque, New Mexico
87110
505/766-3430

New York
26 Federal Plaza
Room 29-118
New York, New York 10278
212/264-7755

445 Broadway
Room 236-A
Albany, New York 12207
518/472-6300

111 West Huron Street
Room 1311
Buffalo, New York 14202
716/846-4301

333 East Water Street
Room 412
Elmira, New York 14901
607/733-4686

35 Pinelaw Road
Room 102E
Melville, New York 11747
516/454-0764

26 Federal Plaza
Room 3100
New York, New York 10278
212/264-1766

100 State Street
Room 601
Rochester, New York 14614
716/263-6700

100 South Clinton Street
Room 1071
Federal Building
Syracuse, New York 13260
315/423-5382

North Carolina
230 South Tryon Street
Suite 700
Charlotte, North Carolina
28202
704/371-6561

215 South Evans Street
Room 102-E
Greenville, North Carolina
27834
919/752-3798

North Dakota
P.O. Box 3086
657 Second Avenue, North
Fargo, North Dakota 58102
701/237-5131

Ohio
1240 East 9th Street
Room 317
AJC Federal Building
Cleveland, Ohio 44199
216/522-4194

85 Marconi Boulevard
Room 512
Columbus, Ohio 43215
614/469-6860

550 Main Street
Room 5028
Cincinnati, Ohio 45202
513/684-2814

Oklahoma
200 N.W. 5th Street
Suite 670
Oklahoma City, Oklahoma
73102
405/231-5239

333 West Fourth Street
Room 3104
Tulsa, Oklahoma 74103
918/581-7495

Oregon
1220 S.W. Third Avenue
Room 676
Federal Building
Portland, Oregon
97204-2882
503/423-5221

Pennsylvania
One Bala Cynwyd Plaza
231 St. Asaphs Road
Suite 640, West Lobby
Bala Cynwyd, Pennsylvania
19004
215/596-5889

One Bala Cynwyd Plaza
231 St. Asaphs Road
Suite 400, East Lobby
Bala Cynwyd, Pennsylvania
19004
215/596-3311

100 Chestnut Street
Room 309
Harrisburg, Pennsylvania
17101
717/782-3840

960 Penn Avenue
Convention Tower, 5th Floor
Pittsburgh, Pennsylvania
15222
412/644-5441

Penn Place
20 North Pennsylvania Ave.
Wilkes-Barre, Pennsylvania
18702
717/826-6497

Puerto Rico
Federal Building, 6th Floor
Carlos Chardon Avenue
Hato Rey, Puerto Rico 00919
809/753-4422

Rhode Island
380 Westminster Mall
Providence, Rhode Island
02903
401/528-4586

South Carolina
1835 Assembly Street
3rd Floor
P.O. Box 2786
Columbia, South Carolina
29201
803/765-5376

South Dakota
101 South Main Avenue
Suite 101
Sioux Falls, South Dakota
57102-0577
605/336-2980

Tennessee
404 James Robertson
Parkway
Suite 1012
Nashville, Tennessee 37219
615/251-5881

Texas
Federal Building
Room 780
300 East 8th Street
Austin, Texas 78701
512/482-7811

400 Mann Street
Suite 403
P.O. Box 9253
Corpus Christi, Texas 78401
512/888-3331

8625 King George Drive
Building C
Dallas, Texas 75235-3391
214/767-7643

1100 Commerce Street
Room 3C36
Dallas, Texas 75242
214/767-0495

10737 Gateway West
Suite 320
El Paso, Texas 79902
915/541-7560

222 East Van Buren Street
Suite 500
Harlingen, Texas 78550
512/423-4533

2525 Murthworth
Houston, Texas 77054
713/660-4409

1611 10th Street
Suite 200
Lubbock, Texas 79401
806/743-7466

100 South Washington Street
Room G-12
Marshall, Texas 75670
214/935-5257

727 East Durango Street
Room A-513
Federal Building
San Antonio, Texas 78206
512/229-6272

Utah
125 South State Street
Room 2237
Salt Lake City, Utah
84138-1195
801/524-3209

Vermont
87 State Street
Room 205
Montpelier, Vermont 05602
802/229-0538

Virginia
400 North 8th Street
Room 3015
P.O. Box 10126
Richmond, Virginia 23240
804/771-2765

Virgin Islands
Veterans Drive
Room 283
St. Thomas, Virgin Islands
00801
809/774-8530

P.O. Box 4010
Christiansted, Virgin Islands
00820
809/773-3480

Washington
Fourth & Vine Building
Room 440
2615 Fourth Avenue
Seattle, Washington 98121
206/442-5677

915 Second Avenue
Room 1792
Seattle, Washington 98174
206/442-8405

651 U.S. Courthouse
P.O. Box 2167
Spokane, Washington 99210
509/456-3781

West Virginia
168 West Main Street
6th Floor
Clarksburg, West Virginia
26301
304/623-5631

Charleston National Plaza
Suite 628
Charleston, West Virginia
25301
304/347-5220

Wisconsin
500 South Barstow Street
Room 17
Eau Claire, Wisconsin 54701
715/834-9012

212 East Washington Ave.
Room 213
Madison, Wisconsin 53703
608/264-5205

310 West Wisconsin Avenue
Room 420
Milwaukee, Wisconsin 53203
414/291-3942

Wyoming
P.O. Box 2839
100 East B Street
Casper, Wyoming
82602-2839
307/261-5761

16

GETTING STARTED: 75 BUSINESSES YOU CAN START TODAY WITHOUT LEAVING HOME!

You probably already know the nature of the business which you intend to operate out of your home. In the event that you don't — or are willing to change your mind — wc offer 75 home business ideas to stimulate your own ideas. Some of them have short descriptions attached; other don't. Each of these ideas can be implemented without leaving home!

Accessories: People love to accessorize everything from cars to clothing.

Advertising

Animals: Breed them or board them. Both are fast-growing business opportunities.

Antiques

Appraisals

Art

Automobile services
Baby items
Beauty services
Bed & Breakfast: The ultimate home-based business. Boarding and feeding guests under your own roof.
Bees: Bee-keeping is increasingly popular — and profitable.
Billing
Bookkeeping
Books
Calligraphy: Good penmanship can pay off!
Camps: Advising others about them.
Careers: Ditto.
Catering
Children's services
Cleaning
Clipping: Gathering news items mentioning people and products.
Clothing
College services
Collecting: If you collect it, someone else will want to buy it.
Computer services
Cooking
Consulting services
Cosmetics
Crafts: Perhaps the original home-based business.
Data Processing
Dating service
Delivery service
Design service
Desktop publishing: Fast-growing, computer-based business providing "instant" publications for business and organizations.

Driving services
Editorial services
Entertainment services: From organizing birthday parties to corporate conventions.
Fashion
Furniture
Hobbies: Your hobby can become the basis of a profit-making business if enough others share your interest.
Household services
Import-Export
Instructional services: Teaching everything from knitting to karate!
Invent something
Jewelry
Lawncare
Liquidation: Garage sales, flea markets, etc.
Mail order
Music
Newsletter publishing
Personal trainer: If you're in good shape, there will be others wanting you to help them shape up.
Pet services
Photo services
Planning services
Plants
Production services
Public relations
Rentals
Repairs
Research
Sales
Secretarial services
Shopping service

Sitting services: House-sitting, baby-sitting, etc.
Special services: Anything you can create in search of a market.
Telephone answering
Translation services
Travel service
Tutoring
Typesetting
Video service
Visiting service: Hospital, homes for the aged, etc.
Wedding services
Word processing
Zoning counseling: The perfect ending to this list!

17

THE SECRET TO SUCCESSFULLY WORKING AT HOME

Hopefully, you have reached the point of seriously considering the possibility of operating a business out of your home.

If you have, you might be wondering if there is some sort of "secret" to success as a home-based entrepreneur.

There is no magic secret that we know of, but we have developed a very short formula which will remind you of three of the primary ingredients which will, at the very least, increase your chances of succeeding as a home-based businessperson. We call it **"The Home Office Entrepreneur's ESP:"**

Energy: You will need mega-doses of stamina to succeed.

Support: You will need the support of your family to succeed.

Perspective: You will need the ability to make constant — and mostly correct — value judgments every working day.

We wish you the best of luck at taking control of your business and personal life under the same roof!

ABOUT THE AUTHOR

Steve Kahn is an attorney and entrepreneur. As an entrepreneur, he has created new businesses in publishing, cable television and real estate. He has been the Executive Producer of "The Miss American Teen-Ager Pageant" for the ABC Television Network and a feature columnist for The New York Times Syndicate with a weekly audience of ten million Sunday newspaper readers. As an attorney, he served as Special Counsel and Director of Investor Relations for the Tishman Real Estate & Construction Co., Inc. He holds a B.S. degree from New York University and a J.D. degree from New York Law School.

ABOUT THE NO NONSENSE
SUCCESS SERIES

More people than ever before are thinking about going into business for themselves — and the No Nonsense Success Guides have been created to provide useful information for this growing and ambitious audience. Look for these related No Nonsense Success Guides: *The Self-Employment Test...Getting Into The Mail Order Business... How To Own And Operate A Franchise... How (and Where) To Get The Money To Get Started ... Getting Into The Consulting Business.*